12.50

DATE DUE

KHOEKHOE

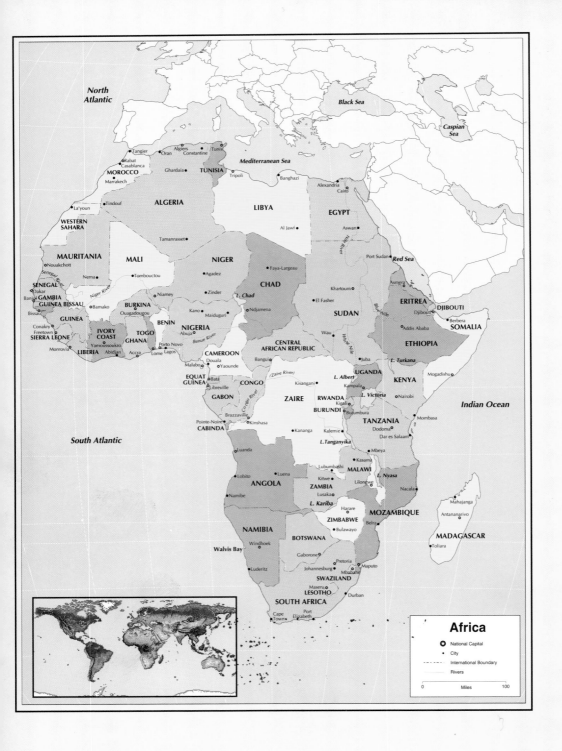

North
Atlantic

Black Sea

Caspian
Sea

Tangier
Rabat
Casablanca
MOROCCO
Marrakech

Oran
Algiers
Constantine
Tunis
TUNISIA

Mediterranean Sea

Ghardaia

Tripoli

Banghazi

Alexandria
Cairo

La'youn
Tindouf

ALGERIA

LIBYA

EGYPT

WESTERN
SAHARA

Tamanrasset

Al Jawf

Aswan

MAURITANIA

MALI

NIGER

Faya-Largeau

Port Sudan

Red Sea

Nouakchott

Nema

Tombouctou

Agadez

CHAD

Khartoum

Asmera

ERITREA

DJIBOUTI

SENEGAL
Dakar
Banjul GAMBIA
GUINEA BISSAU
Bissau

Niger River

Niamey

Zinder

L. Chad

Ndjamena

El Fasher

Djibouti

Berbera

SOMALIA

Bamako

BURKINA
Ouagadougou

Kano
Maiduguri

SUDAN

Wau

Addis Ababa

ETHIOPIA

GUINEA
Conakry
Freetown
SIERRA LEONE
Monrovia
LIBERIA

IVORY
COAST
Yamoussoukro
Abidjan

BENIN
TOGO
GHANA
Accra
Lome

NIGERIA
Abuja
Porto Novo
Lagos

Benue River

CENTRAL
AFRICAN REPUBLIC

Bangui

Juba

White Nile

Blue Nile

L. Turkana

EQUAT
GUINEA
Bata
Libreville

CAMEROON
Malabo
Douala
Yaounde

CONGO

GABON

ZAIRE

(Zaire River)

Kisangani

L. Albert
UGANDA
Kampala

RWANDA
Kigali
BURUNDI
Bujumbura

L. Victoria

Nairobi

KENYA

Mogadishu

Indian Ocean

South Atlantic

Brazzaville
Kinshasa
Pointe-Noire
CABINDA

Congo River

Kananga

Kalemie

TANZANIA
Dodoma
Dar es Salaam

Mombasa

L. Tanganyika

Mbeya

ANGOLA

Luanda

Luena

Lobito

Kasama

Kitwe
Lubumbashi

MALAWI

L. Nyasa

Namibe

ZAMBIA
Lusaka

Lilongwe

Nacala

L. Kariba

Harare

MOZAMBIQUE

NAMIBIA

BOTSWANA

ZIMBABWE
Bulawayo

Mahajanga

Antananarivo

MADAGASCAR
Toliara

Walvis Bay

Windhoek

Gaborone

Pretoria

Maputo

Luderitz

Johannesburg
Mbabane

SWAZILAND

Maseru
LESOTHO

Durban

SOUTH AFRICA

Cape
Town

Port
Elizabeth

Belra

Africa

✪ National Capital

• City

- - - International Boundary

—— Rivers

0   Miles   100

The Heritage Library of African Peoples

KHOEKHOE

Frederick N. Anozie, Ph.D.

THE ROSEN PUBLISHING GROUP, INC.
NEW YORK

Published in 1998 by The Rosen Publishing Group, Inc.
29 East 21st Street, New York, NY 10010

Copyright 1998 by The Rosen Publishing Group, Inc.

First Edition

Library of Congress Cataloging-in-Publication Data

Anozie, Frederick N.
    Khoekhoe / Frederick N. Anozie.
      p.   cm. — (The Heritage library of African peoples)
    Includes bibliographical references and index.
    Summary: An introduction to the history, culture, and contemporary life of the Khoekhoe, also known as Khoikhoi or Khoi, people of southern Africa.
    ISBN 0-8239-2007-0
    1. Khoikhoi (African people)—Juvenile literature. [1. Khoikhoi (African people)] I. Title. II. Series.
DT1768.K56A55   1998
968'.004961—dc21   96-45634
                                          CIP
                                          AC

Manufactured in the United States of America

Contents

INTRODUCTION

THERE IS EVERY REASON FOR US TO KNOW something about Africa and to understand its past and the way of life of its peoples. Africa is a rich continent that has for centuries provided the world with art, culture, labor, wealth, and natural resources. It has vast mineral deposits, fossil fuels, and commercial crops.

But perhaps most important is the fact that fossil evidence indicates that human beings originated in Africa. The earliest traces of human beings and their tools are almost two million years old. Their descendants have migrated throughout the world. To be human is to be of African descent.

The experiences of the peoples who stayed in Africa are as rich and as diverse as of those who established themselves elsewhere. This series of books describes their environment, their modes of subsistence, their relationships, and their customs and beliefs. The books present the variety of languages, histories, cultures, and religions that are to be found on the African continent. They demonstrate the historical linkages between African peoples and the way contemporary Africa has been affected by European colonial rule.

Africa is large, complex, and diverse. It encompasses an area of more than 11,700,000 square miles. The United States, Europe, and India could fit easily into it. The sheer size is an indication of the continent's great variety in geography, terrain, climate, flora, fauna, peoples, languages, and cultures.

Much of contemporary Africa has been shaped by European colonial rule, industrialization, urbanization, and the demands of a world economic system. For more than seventy years, large regions of Africa were ruled by Great Britain, France, Belgium, Portugal, and Spain. African peoples from various ethnic, linguistic, and cultural backgrounds were brought together to form colonial states.

For decades Africans struggled to gain their independence. It was not until after World War II that the colonial territories became independent African states. Today, almost all of Africa is ruled by Africans. Large numbers of Africans live in modern cities. Rural Africa is also being transformed, and yet its people still engage in many of their customs and beliefs.

Contemporary circumstances and natural events have not always been kind to ordinary Africans. Today, however, new popular social movements and technological innovations pose great promise for future development.

George C. Bond, Ph.D., Director
Institute of African Studies
Columbia University, New York

The Khoekhoe were among the earliest inhabitants of southern Africa. This woman belongs to a Khoekhoe group called the Nama, who live in Namibia.

1

THE PEOPLE

THE KHOEKHOE (PRONOUNCED COY-COY)
are one of the earliest peoples to inhabit southern Africa. They occupied large parts of the
countries now known as South Africa and
Namibia. Today small Khoekhoe communities
there still preserve their language and aspects of
their culture.

When Europeans visited southern Africa in
the late 1400s and later settled at Cape Town
in 1652, the people they first encountered were
the Khoekhoe. Terrible conflict occurred
between the newcomers and the natives. In most
areas the traditional Khoekhoe way of life was
destroyed by the mid-1800s. This book focuses
on the Khoekhoe before that time.

▼ THE KHOEKHOE AND THE SAN ▼

The Khoekhoe are one of the two oldest indigenous peoples of southern Africa. The other

group is the San. The word *san* comes from the Khoekhoe verb *sa*, which means to gather food and capture animals. It was once a negative term used by the Khoekhoe, whose herd animals were frequently hunted or stolen by the San.

Because the Khoekhoe and the San have so much in common, most experts believe that the two groups share the same cultural roots. Some experts even combine the two names, referring to both groups as the Khoisan.

Until recently, the Khoekhoe have also been known as the Khoikhoi or Khoi. In Khoekhoe languages, the word *khoe* means person. *Khoekhoe* means people of people.

▼ LANGUAGE ▼

Khoisan languages share a large number of clicking sounds, but Khoekhoe languages have fewer clicks than those of the San. Khoekhoe grammar, however, is more complicated. While San languages do not distinguish between genders and have only singular and plural forms, the Khoekhoe languages have three distinct genders (common, masculine, and feminine) and three number forms (singular, dual, and plural). Thus the word *khoe* (person) has the following gender forms: *khoen* (common), *khoeb* (masculine), and *khoes* (feminine). In addition to these singular forms, the dual form for the

The People

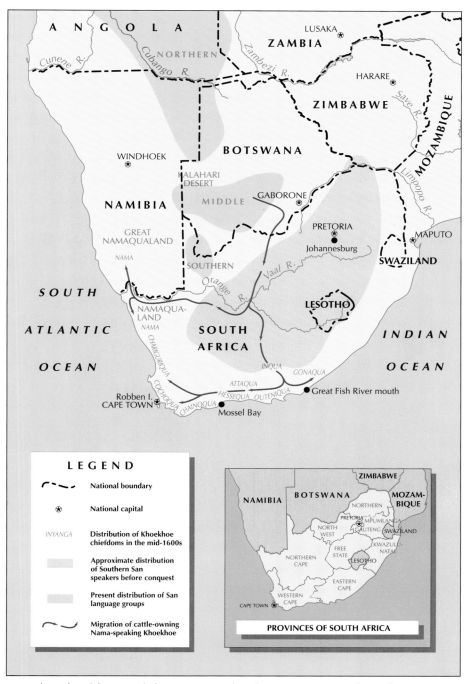

The Khoekhoe and the San once lived in many parts of southern Africa. Today the Nama subgroup of the Khoekhoe in Namibia and parts of South Africa continue to follow many of their traditions and still speak Nama.

feminine gender, for example, is *khoera* (two females) while the plural form is *khoeti* (three or more females). Also, while San languages are very different from each other, the various Khoekhoe languages are closely related.

Clicking languages sound very strange to outsiders. The first Europeans who heard the clicks found them extremely difficult to learn.

▼ INTERACTING WITH OUTSIDE GROUPS ▼

The Khoekhoe and the San share some important history. They were the first indigenous peoples in southern Africa to encounter and regularly resist white settlers. Most of Africa south of the Sahara Desert, including southern Africa, is occupied by Bantu-speaking peoples who are different from the Khoisan in several

This Nama girl lives in Namibia.

Many Khoekhoe and San communities intermarried with Bantu populations. Seen here are children from different backgrounds at a school in Namibia.

ways. The Bantu languages are all broadly related and quite different from the Khoisan click languages. Bantu peoples are generally larger in stature and darker than the Khoisan, and farming played a large role in the traditional economy of most Bantu-speakers. The Bantu peoples of southern Africa came into regular contact and conflict with Europeans much later than the Khoisan.

The Khoekhoe and the San also experienced conflict with the black, Bantu-speaking peoples. However, in many cases the San and Khoekhoe regularly traded with these black societies or intermarried with them. Their closest contact was with the Xhosa people of the present-day

The San were forced to live in the most arid regions of southern Africa. Seen here is a San homestead in the Kalahari Desert.

Eastern Cape province of South Africa. One-sixth of all words in the Xhosa language contain clicks that come from Khoisan languages. Many Xhosa clans are of Khoekhoe origin.

Over several centuries, however, those San and Khoekhoe who remained independent of these dominant black and white communities were forced by them into the most arid and least desirable parts of southern Africa. The San in particular were often targeted for abuse or killed outright. Today only a few San communities remain, mostly in the Kalahari Desert region.

Many Khoekhoe and San were absorbed into other dominant groups. As a result the culture of the Khoekhoe has changed radically over the past 450 years. Khoekhoe who accepted Xhosa

Many people in the Eastern Cape province of South Africa are of Khoekhoe descent. These children from the Eastern Cape display toy windmills, which they have made from metal.

authority became part of Xhosa society. Khoekhoe who mixed with white settlers formed new populations. These include the Coloreds, Griquas, and Korannas in South Africa and the Basters in Namibia. Apart from these large and important populations with strong Khoekhoe roots, a small group of Khoekhoe called the Nama still live in Namibia today. Khoekhoe are also found in the Namaqualand region of the Northern Cape province of South Africa. There they live mainly in the arid reserves of Richtersveld, Leliefontein, Komaggas, and Steinkopf. Some of them still speak the Nama language.

These various groups of Khoekhoe descendants all live under very different circumstances

Many Khoekhoe still live in the Northern Cape province of South Africa
in arid reserves such as the Richtersveld (above).

today. It is therefore not accurate to speak about
them as if they were one population. Instead,
this book focuses on what is known about
Khoekhoe life in the past in order to understand
the heritage that is shared by people of
Khoekhoe descent today.▲

chapter

2

EARLY HISTORY

▼ ORIGINS ▼

It is quite likely that San hunter-gatherers are directly related to the very early humans who once lived in many parts of South Africa. Most experts now believe that the first Khoekhoe were San who began to herd sheep about 2,000 years ago.

The change in lifestyle—from foraging to herding—most likely occurred when the San first came into contact with Bantu-speaking herders. In return for working for the herders, the San were probably paid in sheep. These San who first owned herd animals became the Khoekhoe. They began to move regularly to find seasonal pastures for their sheep and later, cattle and goats. In doing so, they established fixed seasonal migration routes.

Over many centuries Khoekhoe and San lifestyles became quite different. A few experts

17

Experts believe that the first Khoekhoe people were San who began to herd sheep (above).

therefore treat the two groups as separate, although they agree that there has been frequent trade, marriage, and other contact between them over the centuries.

Some experts believe that the similar physical characteristics between the San and Khoekhoe prove that the two groups are related. Most San are small and wiry people; most Khoekhoe, however, are taller and larger than the San. This may be a result of their different diets over many centuries. The nutritional value of milk, which was an important food for the Khoekhoe herders, may have boosted their growth. They curdled milk in skin bags until it turned into a yogurt-like substance.

The San and the Khoekhoe also have similar traditional weapons and tools, cooking utensils, and ornaments.

Sheep bones discovered in archaeological excavations suggest that the Khoekhoe have been in the Cape region for nearly 2,000 years. Around 1300 AD they seem to have acquired cattle, probably from Bantu-speaking herders and farmers who lived in the Eastern Cape. By the mid-1600s these Bantu-speaking groups had formed together into the Xhosa nation. The Xhosa came to dominate the Khoekhoe groups living to the south and west and frequently absorbed them into Xhosa society.

▼ PORTUGUESE ENCOUNTERS ▼

The Khoekhoe's relationships with whites were marred by violence right from the start.

In 1487 a Portuguese explorer named Bartholomeu Dias became the first European to sail around the southern tip of Africa, opening up a European sea route to India. He approached a bay on the east coast of what is now South Africa, where he saw many cattle herded by Khoekhoe. As the strange ships approached, the Khoekhoe fled with their cattle. Dias sailed up the coast a little farther in search of fresh water and food until he came to Mossel Bay. As the Portuguese filled their water barrels, some Khoekhoe approached.

They refused to accept the presents offered
by the Portuguese and began to throw stones.
Dias drew his crossbow and killed a Khoekhoe
man. As far as we know, this was the first
bloodshed between Europeans and the indigenous peoples of South Africa. It was the beginning of South Africa's violent history of racial
conflict.

In 1497 another Portuguese explorer named
Vasco da Gama arrived at Mossel Bay. This time
the Portuguese, while sitting in rowboats in the
surf, offered bells and caps to the Khoekhoe. In
return, the Khoekhoe gave them ivory bangles.
The Khoekhoe began to play on flutes and
dance. The Portuguese blew their trumpets and
danced too. Since all seemed to be going well,
the Portuguese landed and traded three
Portuguese bracelets for an ox.

The Portuguese stayed for thirteen days.
Without asking permission, they took water from
the Khoekhoe's stream. Since rights to water and
land were the key to the Khoekhoe's sense of
ownership, the Portuguese were committing an
offense. The Khoekhoe expressed their anger and
drove their cattle out of sight. Thinking a battle
was about to occur, Da Gama ordered the can-
nons to be fired. The Khoekhoe fled.

The first Portuguese man actually to land at
Cape Town itself was Antonio de Saldanha in
1503. He, too, needed fresh water for his sailors.

About 200 Khoekhoe attacked the Portuguese as they prepared to leave, wounding De Saldanha.

In 1510 a Portuguese viceroy named Dom Francisco de Almeida made a similar mistake. An aristocrat and a famous leader, De Almeida was returning to Portugal after destroying the important city of Kilwa in East Africa and winning other victories in the Indian Ocean. The Portuguese landed and took water, and some went to the nearby Khoekhoe village to trade for meat. A fight broke out over the transaction, and some Portuguese men were beaten. This event provoked De Almeida to lead a party of more than one hundred men ashore to punish the Khoekhoe. He thought guns would be unnecessary, so the men carried only swords and lances.

The Portuguese rowed ashore and attacked the Khoekhoe village, seizing cattle and children. The Khoekhoe cattle were all trained for battle. By whistling and issuing other commands, the Khoekhoe instructed their captured cattle to surround the Portuguese. Many Portuguese were trampled; others fell to the Khoekhoe's slingshots and spears. De Almeida was killed by a spear in the throat. About half of the Portuguese were killed, including several aristocrats. Some Portuguese historians have described this event as the worst disaster in their history, since so many leading men were killed by such a small

Khoekhoe cattle were trained to carry riders and even to fight in battle. Seen above is a drawing from the early 1700s of a Khoekhoe family on the move.

opposing force—perhaps as few as eighty Khoekhoe, excluding the cattle. This disaster confirmed the Portuguese suspicion that the Cape should be avoided.

▼ KHOEKHOE AND THE ENGLISH ▼

The Portuguese control of the trade with ports around the Indian Ocean was soon challenged by other nations. The British and the Dutch formed commercial companies to trade in the Indian Ocean. They both saw the Cape as a perfect halfway point for a break on the long voyages from Europe to India.

The city of Cape Town (above) faces Table Bay. The city was founded in 1652 by Dutch settlers.

Table Bay provided a good place to anchor; the climate was healthy, freshwater streams poured off Table Mountain, and there was plenty of food available from the good fishing and abundant wild animals. Also, sheep and cattle could be traded with the Khoekhoe for small pieces of copper and iron, which they valued highly.

Sir Thomas Smythe, who also attempted the first settlement of Virginia in the United States, played a leading role in setting up the British East India Company in 1600. He had heard from British sailors that the Cape was an ideal place to start a settlement. The Khoekhoe were described as very polite and agreeable, even loving, although at first they were afraid of the British because of their prior experiences with other Europeans. However, the Khoekhoe were unhappy whenever Europeans seemed to be settling permanently and would refuse to trade with them.

In 1613 Smythe appears to have ordered a British ship to bring a Khoekhoe leader to England. A Khoekhoe chief known as Coree and a companion were invited aboard a British ship at the Cape, which set sail without warning. The two Khoekhoe were extremely alarmed and anxious. One died soon after the journey began; the other, Coree, was taken to live with Smythe.

The Khoekhoe chief was treated very well in England and given several gifts. Nevertheless he wanted to return to his home. He lay on the floor every day and cried in broken English for home. Eventually he was taken back to the Cape, where he immediately threw off all the fancy English clothes he had been given and returned to his familiar sheepskin clothing.

The British soon came to regret kidnapping Coree, because the Khoekhoe quickly raised their prices on trade goods. Before Coree's trip to England, the British had been able to trade some brass, cut out of two or three old kettles, for thirty-nine oxen and 115 sheep. Afterward they had to produce many very fine kettles to get any cattle. Prices also went up because more

CLOTHING

Traditionally Khoekhoe women wore pointed skin caps, which were often decorated with beads and tassles, and leggings made from strips of leather. They often carried leather bags that hung down their backs. They also wore earrings made from small pieces of metal. Men's caps were more helmet-like. Men wore small copper plates, European coins, small white horns, and large coral beads in their hair. Both men and women also wore karosses, or cloaks made from animal skin. The Khoekhoe disliked European clothing and thought it was ridiculous.

This drawing from the 1700s shows a Khoekhoe couple wearing traditional clothing.

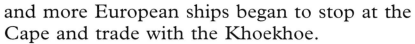

and more European ships began to stop at the
Cape and trade with the Khoekhoe.

Coree remained a valuable contact for the
British. He was proud of his trip and even
planned to return to England with his son.
Smythe attempted to establish a small settlement
of ten British convicts at the Cape. While the
ships waited, the men set out to find Coree. One
was killed, and another was wounded on the
way. Coree immediately came to the shore and
demanded an explanation of why the men were
being stationed there.

The British offered to build Coree an
English-style house if he would let the men stay.
He agreed, on the condition that the British
supply the men with muskets and allow Coree
to use the men as soldiers to attack his enemies.
Coree's reaction suggests that although the
Khoekhoe were against anyone settling on their
land, they were eager to advance themselves at
the expense of their local enemies.

Coree's plan did not seem safe to the British,
so the convicts were sent to live on Robben
Island instead. Later this island became the infa-
mous prison where President Nelson Mandela
and other South African political prisoners were
sent. Robben Island was a kind of prison for the
ten British convicts too: it had no trees or shel-
ter, no fresh water, and it was full of rats and
poisonous snakes. These Englishmen had nearly

This view from the top of Table Mountain shows some of the suburbs of Cape Town. Robben Island is near the top of the picture.

lost their minds by the time other passing ships took pity on them and returned the survivors to Europe.

In addition to its trading function, the Cape also served as a mail station, where ships could leave letters about their voyages and share information. In about 1631 the British took aboard another Khoekhoe captain called

Autshumato. Autshumato was the captain of a poor beachcombing clan and had many enemies among the Cape Khoekhoe. The British took him on a voyage to the East, nicknamed him Harry, and taught him English. Autshumato was returned to the Cape to act as postmaster and translator. For many decades he was the key middleman between Europeans and the Khoekhoe at the Cape.

▼ THE KHOEKHOE AND THE DUTCH ▼

In 1652 the Dutch East India Company, known by its Dutch initials VOC, established the first permanent European settlement in southern Africa. The VOC settlement was set up to provide food for passing ships. The Dutch commander, Jan van Riebeeck, was instructed to treat the Khoekhoe fairly and pay them properly for items traded. Earlier Dutch sailors had found that this ensured good relations. Unfortunately, Van Riebeeck was prejudiced against the Khoekhoe, and relations quickly deteriorated.

When the Dutch arrived, the Khoekhoe clans they encountered at the port of Cape Town included the Goringhaicona, the Gorachoqua, and the Goringhaiqua. A stronger group called the Chainoqua had many cattle and lived beyond the Hottentots Holland Mountains. The largest group in the southwestern Cape was the Cochoqua.

PREJUDICE AGAINST THE KHOEKHOE

Of all the peoples that early European visitors encountered in Africa, the Khoekhoe were one of the least understood. Many aspects of their culture were very foreign to Europeans: their clicking language; their minimal clothing; their nomadic lifestyle and portable houses; their diet; and their habit of shining their skin with animal fat. As a result, Europeans developed many unfair prejudices about the Khoekhoe. They called the Khoekhoe Hottentots, a name derived from the word the Khoekhoe chanted during their dances of welcome and celebration.

In the Western view, the label Hottentot came to be associated with the lowest forms of human life, and it was used as a racial slur against anyone who was regarded as inferior or "primitive." In fact, the Khoekhoe were neither. They were relatively peaceful people who were willing to share and trade their resources according to certain rules. The Europeans and the Khoekhoe did not understand each other's traditions. Before the Europeans had proper knowledge of Khoekhoe culture, they developed negative views about the Khoekhoe people. Also, the Europeans wanted cattle from the Khoekhoe and rights to the land that the Khoekhoe had occupied for centuries. As a result of the Europeans' ambitions, the Khoekhoe experienced great cruelty and hostility under white authority.

Among all the insulting, ignorant, and often false accounts of the Khoekhoe by early travelers, several sources praise their intelligence, expressiveness, bravery, athletic agility, expert fighting and hunting skills, and general good humor.

Other Khoekhoe lived in the southeastern
and northwestern Cape, and eastward along the
Cape coast as far as the Great Fish River. They
also lived along the Orange River and in several
parts of Namibia, from where some experts
believe they may have migrated southward centuries before.

Khoekhoe herders generally occupied land
that was unsuitable for the farming of African
crops, which required summer rainfall. Since
much of the Western Cape, Northern Cape,
and Namibia are arid or receive winter rain,
there was little competition for this land with
Bantu herders, who also farmed. However, when
whites arrived, the Khoekhoe suddenly faced
competition for much of this territory.

The Khoekhoe were expert at making a living
from their environment. They migrated with the
seasons to take advantage of the best grazing
conditions and available water. Various clans
held the rights to particular pastures and water
sources, but they did not have the same ideas
about land ownership as the Europeans did.
Land could not be sold, but temporary rights
to the land could be negotiated. Some of the
Dutch began to think that they owned parts of
the land on which they settled. Others thought
they had purchased land from Khoekhoe in
return for gifts. In the Khoekhoe view, the gifts
only secured temporary rights to water and

This Namibian girl is carrying a bag of oranges on her head.

grazing. These widely different views about resources resulted in much conflict.

Events of the following decades at the Cape
changed the lives of the Khoekhoe forever.
Those events set in motion patterns of colonial
behavior that greatly influenced the history of
South Africa.▲

chapter

3

TRADITIONS

TODAY WE CAN FORM A PICTURE OF WHAT
Khoekhoe life was like when the first settlers
arrived in the mid-1600s. Our ideas are based
on the oral history of modern Khoekhoe communities, settlers' records, and modern research.

▼ SOCIETY ▼

The basis of Khoekhoe society was the
extended family. At the center of the family was
the head male, who could have several wives.
Several extended families made up the clan,
which shared the same corral, or kraal, where
they kept their livestock. Kraal was also the
name given to the settlement or temporary
village.

Members of a clan were all related to the
same distant ancestor, and they could not marry
each other. Clan members shared the same
territory, grazing grounds, and water sources.

WHY THE DEAD WILL REMAIN DEAD

One day Heiseb said, "We are starving. There is no food in this terrible place. We must move away." He took his wife and son to a new region, where berries covered the bushes and fell to the ground. His son rushed forward to gather them, but Heiseb stopped him, saying, "These berries are for grown-ups only, not for greedy children."

Heiseb's son begged, "Please let me have some. Look, I'm dying of hunger. See, I am dead!" He fell down and pretended to be dead. Heiseb said, "For the dead, there is only burial," and he buried him there.

In the morning Heiseb's son secretly got up from his grave, but when he spotted his mother in the distance, he lay back down in his grave.

One day his sorrowful mother came to the grave, but her son was not there. She looked for him everywhere because she wanted to take him home. She said, "I will wait for my son behind this tree because he is alive, and surely he will come again." Her son, glancing around cautiously, saw no one and came slowly back to the grave. Then his mother jumped out from her hiding place and said "My son, oh, my son! I have found you!" She embraced him happily. And when they arrived home she said, "In the grave there is life! Oh, the joy of it! Look Heiseb, our son is still alive!"

But Heiseb said, "I thought my son was dead, so I buried him; but it appears that he is still alive. Nevertheless, the dead will remain dead." At that point, Heiseb got up and killed his son.

So it is that to this day people die and are dead; and in the grave there is only death.

(Khoekhoe Nama fable, from E. W. Thomas, *Bushman Stories*, Oxford Univ. Press, 1949.)

They also spoke the same dialect of the Khoekhoe language.

Respected men, and occasionally women, were chosen as clan captains. Captains settled disputes and made major decisions for the group.

The chief, or *kouqui*, was the head of the senior clan. Together with other clan captains he made decisions affecting the chiefdom, which generally consisted of 1,000 to 2,000 people in the mid-1600s.

Khoekhoe chiefdoms were quite flexible. If a group grew too large or grazing became scarce, some clans split off and formed new chiefdoms. In their seasonal migrations, the Khoekhoe sometimes absorbed smaller bands of peoples, such as groups of San. If the Khoekhoe lost their herds to raids or natural causes, they were sometimes forced to turn to hunting and gathering like the San. Sometimes Khoekhoe groups controlled groups of Bantu-speakers, but more often the opposite occurred. Several Khoekhoe chiefdoms became Xhosa clans.

▼ THE *KOUQUI* ▼

The office of *kouqui* passed from father to son. If a chief had no son, the title was passed to his next oldest brother or nephew. Succession by females was strictly forbidden. A new *kouqui* was installed when the old one died or resigned.

During his installation, the new *kouqui* stood before an assembly of clan captains and formally promised to preserve all the laws and customs of his people. He then slaughtered some sheep or an ox to provide meat for a feast in honor of the captains. The broth was given to their wives. After the main feast, the *kouqui*'s wife prepared another feast for the captains' wives. At this meal, the women ate the meat, and their husbands drank the broth.

The *kouqui* presided over the community council, which consisted of the kraal captains. This was the main governing body of the community. The *kouqui* summoned the council only when important matters affecting the community arose. The captains met in the residence of the *kouqui*, and seated themselves in a circle around the *kouqui*. The council's proceedings were very democratic. The *kouqui* neither imposed his will on the council nor treated it as a group of advisors. His main role was to direct the discussion of members and to summarize the opinions of the majority at the end. Everyone, including the *kouqui*, was bound by the decision of the majority.

In the past the community council decided matters of war and peace and determined relations with other groups. The chief led his chiefdom in battle. Today the functions of the council (where it has survived) are limited to

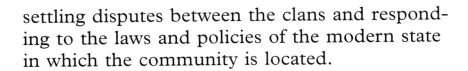

settling disputes between the clans and responding to the laws and policies of the modern state in which the community is located.

▼ CAPTAINS ▼

Like the *kouqui*, a kraal captain made a formal promise, and he and his wife also prepared feasts for family heads and their wives. The kraal council functioned much like the community council, but it had greater powers over the local affairs of its members. It made decisions about moving to new grazing grounds, using water resources, and scheduling and organizing feasts and celebrations. The kraal council settled disputes among its own members. It also tried criminal cases and imposed sentences. In all these matters, the kraal council did not have to answer to the community council. However, in times of war, the kraal captain led his troops under the command of the *kouqui*.

This system of government was like the United States' federal democratic system, which gives great control to local communities.

▼ KHOEKHOE SETTLEMENTS ▼

Because of their nomadic lifestyle, the Khoekhoe had housing that was easy to move. When it was time to move with the herds, the house could be taken apart and carried on the backs of oxen.

These details of two early sketches at the Cape both show traditional Khoekhoe houses in the foreground. The houses consisted of a framework of bent branches, over which mats were placed. They could be easily taken down and transported on the back of an ox. In the background of the top picture workers are stacking hay. In the background of the bottom picture are European-style houses.

Khoekhoe houses were dome-shaped. Their frames were made from bent saplings, or small trees. Soon after they were cut, the saplings were secured into the ground in a circular pattern. The saplings were then pulled together so that they met in the middle, and they remained bent when dry. Several beautifully stitched grass mats were then placed over this framework. Each mat had a different name and a particular place upon the framework. Women assembled the covering of the house by placing each mat in its assigned place.

These kinds of houses are still built today by Khoekhoe people in Namaqualand, in the Northern Cape province of South Africa. They call the houses *matjieshuise*, meaning houses made from small mats.

The Khoekhoe settlement, or kraal, consisted of a number of homes. Some kraals remained in use for several years if there was enough grazing land and water in the area. In the mid-1600s one Khoekhoe chief who settled near the Olifants River had over 4,000 cattle and 3,000 sheep in his kraal.

▼ THE IMPORTANCE OF CATTLE ▼

Cattle were the cornerstone of the Khoekhoe economy and the measure of personal wealth. Cattle were seldom eaten, except for special ceremonies, such as marriages. They were an important source of milk products, including butter and fat.

Fat was a sign of wealth and all the goodness of life. The Khoekhoe word for fat is the same as the word for rich. This explains why the Khoekhoe scraped the fat off Europeans' cooking pots and applied it to their bodies. The fat also protected their skin from sunburn. Similar customs are followed by many other herding societies in Africa. If people cannot afford to anoint themselves with butter or fat from their flocks, herds, or other sources, it is a sure sign that food is scarce.

The Khoekhoe covered their bodies in fat mixed with red ocher, a mineral obtained from the earth. Some Khoekhoe mixed sweet-smelling herbs called *buku* into their ocher grease. *Buku* and a shiny, silver-colored mineral called specularite were worn by some Khoekhoe in their hair. Like fat, this shininess was regarded as beautiful. Yellow and white ocher were used for face painting. In addition to decorating the body, these items were also traded.

When animals were slaughtered, the Khoekhoe identified with the valued animal by draping its entrails around their shoulders. They also ate every part of the animal including the innards that Europeans discarded. Europeans found all these habits disgusting. Likewise the Khoekhoe thought that the Europeans were wasteful.

Khoekhoe cattle were of the humpbacked kind seen here.

Each Khoekhoe family owned its own livestock and pastured its animals together with
those of other families from the settlement. Men
were in charge of looking after and training the
cattle herd, while women and boys took care of
the other animals. Their cattle descended from
the long-horned, humpbacked kind that were
first introduced to Africa from Asia more than
2,000 years ago.

Since there were so many animals in a settlement, the Khoekhoe marked the animals to tell
them apart. For example, the ear of an animal
could be pierced in a certain way as a sign of
ownership. In some cases the color of the animals was also an indication of ownership. A
family that owned mainly white cattle would
sometimes exchange brown calves with a
neighbor whose stock was mainly brown.

There were several ways to acquire cattle.
Parents could give or bequeath livestock to their

young sons. Young men from poorer families,
or poor adults who had either lost or never pos-
sessed livestock, could earn animals as payment
for herding a richer man's livestock. Craftsmen
and other professionals, such as doctors, could
also barter their goods or services for animals.
The most dramatic way of acquiring livestock
was by raiding neighbors or other peoples settled
farther away.

Cattle raiding among the Khoekhoe goes back
several centuries and was regarded as an honor-
able enterprise—a test of manhood, skill, and
bravery. It required considerable athletic and
mental skills to successfully break into other
people's kraals, seize their cattle, and return
home unharmed. Men also had to defend their
own kraals against outside attackers. Sometimes
hostages were captured and then ransomed for
cattle. Khoekhoe herds were most often attacked
by San hunters, for whom both wild animals
and stock herds were considered fair game.
Considerable hostility developed between the
two groups as a result. Many San rock paintings
record such raids.

▼ ECONOMY ▼

The Khoekhoe mainly ate sheep and goats.
Khoekhoe sheep were fat-tailed, with scraggly
hair rather than the woolly type. Khoekhoe
made soft clothing with the sheepskin and

In the past Khoekhoe women sewed fine leather clothing, which they sometimes decorated with beads. The Nama woman above belongs to a Namibian woman's group that makes beautifully embroidered cloths. The schoolchildren below live in the Eastern Cape.

occasionally used finer furs for fancy garments worn by people of higher rank. Like the San, the Khoekhoe hunted game and gathered wild plants as a source of nutrition. The Khoekhoe kept dogs for hunting. They used bows and poisoned arrows, the knobkerrie (a kind of throwing club), and various types of traps, especially pitfall traps. This equipment was similar to that used by their San and Bantu-speaking neighbors. As iron became more readily available through trade, the Khoekhoe and the San quickly adopted iron-tipped weapons.

Some Khoekhoe clans spent seasons at the coast and harvested food from the ocean shore. As a result, fewer animals from the Khoekhoe flocks had to be slaughtered for food. If a clan lost its cattle, they would look for food along the seashore. Observing these people searching for food, the Dutch named them *strandlopers*, or beachcombers. Women collected shellfish along the rocky coastline; men hunted seals. The fat from the seals was especially important to several Khoekhoe groups.

Khoekhoe clans traded with one another, with the San (who were known as Soaqua in the Cape), and with Bantu-speaking communities. Trade items included foods, ostrich eggshell beads, pottery, and animal skins, furs, and horns. Scarce items like iron, produced by black peoples far to the north, and a few European

beads were also traded. Copper from Namaqualand was very highly valued. It was traded in small pieces or as decorations.

Another important trade item was the plant called *dagga*, which contains an intoxicating drug and can induce hallucinations. It can also be used to enhance the experience of sacredness in religious dances and celebrations and to help people enter trance states. In recent

Dancing was an important social activity among the Khoekhoe. The sketches on this page and on the facing page all show Khoekhoe women dancing. Women clapped to the rhythm of the music.

times the word *dagga* has become identified with marijuana, an imported substance that has largely replaced the original, indigenous drug. The Attaqua clan, who lived between present-day George and Knysna, were mentioned by early settlers as growers of this valued drug.

Deze heeft 2 Groffen aen.

▼ **MEDICINE** ▼
Europeans were amazed at the medical skills of the Khoekhoe. The Khoekhoe often were asked to treat sailors with broken bones or illnesses that European doctors could not cure. The Khoekhoe used a wide variety of herbs and medicinal plants that are used today in Western medicines.▲

Hier is de zak op 'e rug met een quast.

chapter

4

COLONIAL HISTORY

THE FIRST DECADES OF THE VOC'S CAPE
settlement greatly affected the future of the
Khoekhoe. The Khoekhoe's strategies of resisting and frustrating the Dutch nearly caused
them to abandon their settlement. But in the
end the Khoekhoe did not exert enough pres-
sure to force the Dutch off their land.

Instead the Khoekhoe tried to turn the situa-
tion to their advantage by adapting to changes
and new opportunities. The lives of the Cape
Khoekhoe were quickly changed forever, while
those far from the Cape were not significantly
affected until centuries later. Khoekhoe figures
who played key roles in the early years of the
Cape settlement show the different ways in
which the Khoekhoe responded to change.

▼ THE SUPPLY STATION ▼
The voyage between Europe and India lasted
from six to eight months. Sailors endured filthy

Seen here are Nama leaders Samuel Isaak (left) and
Hendrik Witbooi (second left)

A Nama woman,
photographed around 1905.

The Nama and other Khoekhoe peoples in Namibia played a leading role in resisting German
colonial rule in Namibia, which was imposed in the late 1800s. Two heroes of the Nama resis-
tance were Samuel Isaak (seen with his wife at bottom right) and Hendrik Witbooi, who was
killed in action in 1905. These two men are still honored today (bottom left).

conditions, brutal treatment, and sickness and disease (particularly scurvy, which resulted from the lack of vitamin C). The VOC's intention in sending the Dutch commander Jan van Riebeeck with one hundred men to the Cape was to supply ships with both fresh meat and produce. The settlement was at first a failure in this regard.

Once the Khoekhoe realized that trading animals allowed the Europeans to remain at the Cape, they refused to trade with them. Animals equaled wealth to the Khoekhoe, so naturally they did not want the Dutch to have them. At first they did not understand that the Dutch economy did not revolve around cattle.

After seven months Van Riebeeck had managed to obtain only three cows and four sheep. The Dutch were unskilled at hunting wild animals; some colonists were even killed by lions outside the fort. Soon the Dutch were forced by hunger to capture penguins and club seals on Robben Island for meat, just as the poorest Khoekhoe clans sometimes did. The crops they planted struggled to grow.

Instead of becoming a rich supply station for passing ships, the Dutch settlement could barely feed itself. It was not living up to its name: the Cape of Good Hope. The Dutch authorities were angry. Meanwhile the Khoekhoe despised the Dutch way of life. They thought the Dutch were slaves to the soil for attempting to farm, and cowards who lived in forts and houses. The Khoekhoe, on the other hand, considered themselves the masters of the land, free to herd their animals wherever they chose.

▼ AUTSHUMATO AND EVA ▼

The Dutch relied on the shrewd Khoekhoe captain and postmaster, Autshumato, for information. They always suspected he was manipulating them to his own advantage, but they needed Autshumato's translating skills.

Autshumato told the Dutch that thousands of Khoekhoe from three large clans would soon arrive at the Cape on their seasonal migration path. The Dutch were fearful but hoped to obtain more animals. One morning they awoke to find their fort surrounded by Khoekhoe herds. However, the Khoekhoe did not want to trade with the Dutch and kept asking Autshumato when the English were coming. The Dutch suspected that Autshumato favored the English and that he bargained up trade prices when translating negotiations.

The Dutch clearly needed alternate Khoekhoe middlemen. The Van Riebeecks decided to take Autshumato's niece, a bright and charming girl who was about ten years old, into their home. They named her Eva and taught her European ways of life. She grew into an attractive and accomplished woman who was fluent in several European languages. She was the first Khoekhoe to be assimilated into European society, and she eventually married a European surgeon. However, for much of her life she was torn between the Dutch and Khoekhoe communities. Eventually she left her husband and was arrested for disorderly conduct.

▼ THE STRUGGLE OVER LAND ▼ AND CATTLE

After eighteen months at the Cape, the Dutch had forty-two cattle and one hundred sheep. One Sunday when the Dutch were praying, their herd boy was murdered and all the cattle were taken. Autshumato and his followers disappeared at the same time. The settlers were outraged. VOC headquarters allowed the Dutch to issue an arrest warrant for Autshumato, but forbade the use of violence. The Dutch had to watch as their precious animals grazed around them, mixing into the Khoekhoe herds. The Khoekhoe now refused to trade, saying that the Dutch were living on their land, not intending to go away, and taking the best grazing land for themselves.

To show their resolve, the Khoekhoe quickly built about fifty houses right beside the fort. They refused to move off their land and threatened to destroy the fort with help from inland clans if the Dutch interfered with them.

This interesting drawing shows a group of Khoekhoe gathered around a fire. The man in the foreground is lighting his pipe with one hand. In the other he holds a flywhisk, a swatter made from a jackal tail.

The Dutch feared that Autshumato was stirring up trouble in the hinterland. An attack by the combined Khoekhoe groups easily would have wiped out the settlement.

To the surprise of the Dutch, Autshumato returned in a state of panic, having no doubt made enemies among the other Khoekhoe clans, who had never liked him. Since they still needed his services, the Dutch forgave Autshumato for the time being. Meanwhile a Khoekhoe man named Doman had confirmed that Autshumato had organized the cattle stealing scheme. Van Riebeeck thought Doman would be a valuable ally. He sent Doman to the Dutch colony of Batavia (present-day Indonesia) to learn the Dutch language and the Christian religion.

▼ FARMERS ▼

Meanwhile the farming attempts of the settlement were improving. The VOC expanded its gardens and wheat fields into more sheltered locations away from windy Table Bay. To extend their occupation of this growing territory, the Dutch decided in 1656 to encourage permanent settlers. The VOC offered former employees and other willing settlers as much land as they wanted for planting gardens. This new class of farmers were called free burghers (meaning free residents in Dutch). The term indicated that they were not contracted VOC employees like everyone else; they were the first people to settle of their own free will.

Many of these farmers began to identify more closely with the Khoekhoe than with the VOC, which used harsh methods to control every aspect of life at the Cape. Farmers quickly realized that the Khoekhoe herding lifestyle was easier and more profitable than farming in the Cape. Although the VOC strictly forbade farmers to trade with the Khoekhoe, a booming black market in a wide range of items soon emerged.

▼ WORKERS, SLAVES, AND RESISTERS ▼

Many Khoekhoe learned Dutch and were willing to work for the white farmers. Overall, however, there were not enough workers, and a labor shortage soon developed at the Cape. Slaves were brought from West Africa and Asia to work on the Dutch farms. Many of these slaves escaped and joined the Khoekhoe.

The Dutch turned to their Khoekhoe middlemen for information about the runaway slaves. Autshumato claimed to know nothing about their whereabouts. Meanwhile Eva warned Van Riebeeck that Doman, who had returned in 1658, was plotting against the Dutch. Doman also claimed to know nothing of the slaves and called Eva a traitor to her people. Van Riebeeck exiled Autshumato to Robben Island. He was the first black leader in South Africa to be imprisoned there. He was also the first of the very few who managed to escape.

The Dutch seized Khoekhoe hostages and demanded that their slaves be returned to them. Doman was outraged and blamed Eva for the decision. In fact, the taking of hostages was an accepted practice among the Khoekhoe. Doman himself had previously recommended that Van Riebeeck hold Autshumato hostage until the Dutch cattle were returned.

Doman had changed his opinions about the Dutch. While in Batavia, he learned the Dutch language, culture, religion, and use of firearms. However, when he returned to the Cape, he immediately rejected everything Dutch and set about using his knowledge against them. He bitterly hated Eva because she chose to collaborate with the Dutch instead of resisting them. In fact, Doman was plotting war.

▼ WAR ▼

Doman was waiting for the beginning of the wet Cape winter. This rainy season dampened the Dutch gunpowder and matches to the point where they were almost useless. Though Eva had warned the Dutch, they could do nothing but wait. As the rains of 1659 began to fall, the Khoekhoe started to attack the settlement.

Farms and houses were destroyed and animals were raided. More and more farmers fled into the fort for safety. Some VOC employees and slaves planned to kill everyone in the fort and escape in a ship. Eva told Van Riebeeck that Doman was planning to kill all the Europeans and would soon scale the fort's walls.

Just when things looked hopeless for the Dutch, Doman was wounded and the hostilities abated. During peace negotiations the Khoekhoe explained their anger at the fact that their land was being stolen from them. If they were to go to Holland, they asked, would they be allowed to take over the land in a similar way? Van Riebeeck replied that the Cape had been won from them in war; it now belonged to the Dutch, and they intended to keep it. In fact, the VOC still had its doubts about keeping the Cape, but the company had invested so much that it did not want to withdraw. A colony had taken root.

In 1672 the VOC persuaded the local Khoekhoe to formally sell the Cape. Khoekhoe farther inland did not agree with the sale. An inland chieftain named Gonnema was a common enemy of the Cape Khoekhoe and the colony. His people and outlying Dutch farmers were continually raiding each other. Soon VOC soldiers, farmers, and Khoekhoe allies were all involved in a four-year war against Gonnema. His greatest defeat came when Cape Khoekhoe led soldiers directly to his camp. Many Cape Khoekhoe were now part of the Dutch settlement; they identifed with it to the extent that they would even fight for the Dutch against rival Khoekhoe clans.

By the mid-1800s, the Cape Khoekhoe had become so mixed with other population groups that they could no longer be told apart. Many people in the Cape, such as these women, have some distant Khoekhoe ancestors.

▼ CHANGES IN KHOEKHOE SOCIETY ▼

At the beginning of the 1700s Cape Town was flourishing. The VOC Gardens, which survive today, were both productive and beautiful.

In 1713 the Cape Khoekhoe were devastated by a smallpox epidemic, which was introduced by a visiting ship. Hundreds died cursing the Dutch; many Khoekhoe survivors fled from the Cape. The surviving Cape Khoekhoe had little choice but to become servants. Many married colonists and Malay slaves, forming what became known as the Cape Coloreds—a classification many of them rejected. By the middle of the 1800s, the Khoekhoe population at the Cape had become so mixed with other groups that the Khoekhoe were no longer distinguishable.

Inland Khoekhoe, on the other hand, had given up the Cape and moved away. White

Those Khoekhoe groups who lived far away from the Cape were less affected by the arrival of the Europeans. They preserved many of their traditions, and their language. These Namibian women still speak the ancient Nama language.

farmers, accompanied by Khoekhoe servants, turned to cattle herding, hunting, raiding, and trading. This brought them into frequent contact with Khoekhoe in the interior, with whom they often traded despite VOC regulations. VOC officials regarded the farmers as cheats who were in direct competition with the VOC for trade with the Khoekhoe, whom officials claimed were being corrupted by European influence.

In the 1700s many Khoekhoe clans dissolved and new alliances were formed. As Xhosa herders moved into Khoekhoe territory in the Eastern Cape from the east, white stock farmers began to move in from the west. Many Khoekhoe clans, such as the Gona, were absorbed by Xhosa-speakers. Many Khoekhoe became the servants of white ranchers; others settled in missionary stations established in the late 1700s.

The Moravian Missionary Society's first missionary among the Khoekhoe was expelled in 1744 after one year. But the Moravians returned in 1792 and established the mission of Genadendal. The London Missionary Society's Dr. Van der Kemp established Bethelsdorp mission in 1799.

Some Khoekhoe mediated disputes between the black and white cattle farmers after they met in the 1770s. The same struggle over the grazing land that the Khoekhoe had first lost to the whites would be repeated in nine frontier wars

This tapestry, made by a Nama woman, shows scenes from Khoekhoe history and daily life. The section at the bottom right shows a battle; at top left an animal is being slaughtered for a feast.

between whites and Xhosa-speakers from 1779 to 1802.

In the late 1700s and early 1800s, many Khoekhoe acquired firearms and horses. Joined by escaped slaves, criminals, and deserters from the Cape colony, groups of mixed ancestry (such as the Griqua and the Kora) sprang up. Some Khoekhoe bands traveled around the countryside raiding weaker groups.

These changes in Khoekhoe society show that the Khoekhoe were extremely adaptable. Both the Khoekhoe at Cape Town and those in the

Today people of Khoekhoe descent are citizens of the modern countries of South Africa and Namibia. The Nama man above wears a patriotic cap.

interior quickly adjusted to new lifestyles and technologies. Only isolated groups, such as the Nama in Namaqualand and Namibia, have preserved aspects of Khoekhoe culture and still follow their traditions today.▲

Glossary

arid Very dry; having insufficient rainfall to support agriculture.

Bantu Group of related peoples who live in the southern African interior and farm for a living; the languages that they speak.

buku Sweet-smelling herb mixed into ochre grease and applied to women's hair.

hinterland Region lying inland from the coast.

Hottentot Insulting label Europeans used to describe the Khoekhoe in the past.

indigenous Local or native to a particular region or environment.

kouqui Khoekhoe chief who headed the senior clan; office was passed from father to son.

kraal Cattle corral, or temporary village.

matjieshuise Houses made from small mats.

ochre Mineral used as a paint or dye.

prejudice A negative opinion formed without just grounds or before sufficient knowledge.

Robben Island Famous prison located off the coast of southern Africa; a group of British convicts was sent there in the 1600s as was Nelson Mandela, current president of South Africa.

voc (Dutch East India Company) Trading business that set up the first permanent settlement in southern Africa.

For Further Reading

Aardema, Verna. *Jackal's Flying Lesson: A Khoikhoi Tale*. New York: Knopf, 1995.

Fairman, Tony. *Bury My Bones But Keep My Words*. New York: Puffin Books, 1991.

Challenging Reading

Barnard, Alan. *Hunters and Herders of Southern Africa: A Comparative Ethnography of the Khoisan Peoples*. London: Cambridge University Press, 1992.

Boonzaier, Emile et al., *The Cape Herders: A History of the Khoikhoi of Southern Africa*. Athens, OH: Ohio University Press, 1996.

Elphick, Richard. *Khoikhoi and the Founding of White South Africa*. Johannesburg: Raven Press, 1985.

Other Resources

Compton's Interactive Encyclopedia 1995. CD-ROM for Windows. Compton's NewMedia, 1994. (Articles on Angola, Botswana, Namibia, and South Africa.)

Index

Index

ACKNOWLEDGMENTS
The publishers are indebted to Professor Henry Bredecamp at the University of the Western Cape for his expert advice on this project. The author extends grateful thanks to Professor Chukwuma Azuonye for contributing to the writing of Chapter 1, and for assisting with supplementary research materials for this book.

ABOUT THE AUTHOR
Dr. Frederick N. Anozie, an archaeologist of prehistoric African cultures, is a senior lecturer and former head of the Department of Archaeology at the University of Nigeria.

PHOTO CREDITS
All photos by Eric L. Wheater except the cover, pp. 8, 42 (top), 57 (top and bottom) by Tony Figueira; pp. 22, 25, 37 (top and bottom), 40, 44 (top and bottom), 45 (top and bottom), and 51 courtesy of the South African Library, Cape Town; p. 47 (all) © National Archives of Namibia, courtesy of Margie Orford; and p. 59 © Helga Kohl.

CONSULTING EDITOR AND LAYOUT
Gary N. van Wyk, Ph.D.

SERIES DESIGN
Kim Sonsky